ASH & CREED PRESS

The Questions of Jesus

Forty devotions

to enrich your Lenten journey

ASH & CREED
PRESS

Bold Stories. Sacred Questions.

Contents

Introduction

Lent is a season of returning—returning to reflection, to hunger, to the quiet places where God meets us without pretense. It is a season shaped not by our strength but by our need. We come as we are: distracted, hopeful, weary, longing. And Jesus meets us with questions.

Throughout the Gospels, Jesus asks far more questions than He answers. His questions are not traps or tests. They are invitations—openings into deeper trust, clearer vision, and honest relationship. He asks in order to draw us near, to awaken desire, to reveal what we cling to and what we fear. His questions are mirrors and doorways, uncovering what is hidden and calling forth what is true.

This devotional follows Jesus's questions from Ash Wednesday to Palm Sunday. The journey is not linear; it is relational. Some questions comfort. Others unsettle. All of them invite us to walk with Him more closely. Lent is not about self-improvement. It is about attention—turning our gaze toward the One who already sees us with compassion.

Each day offers a brief reflection on one of Jesus's questions, followed by two simple elements: an encouragement and a reflection question. The encouragement offers a word of hope or clarity drawn from the day's Scripture. The reflection question is meant to open space—not to close it. Use it as a doorway into prayer, journaling, or quiet contemplation. Let it guide you, but not confine you. This season is not about perfect answers, but about honest attention to the One who asks the questions.

As you walk through these forty days, may the questions of Jesus lead you not into guilt, but into grace; not into striving, but into surrender; not into fear, but into love. May you discover, again and again, that the One who asks is also the One who heals, restores, and calls you by name.

Ash Wednesday, February 18

"What are you seeking?" (John 1:38)

When Jesus turns and asks the first disciples, *"What are you seeking?"* He is not testing them. He is inviting them to name their desire. Lent begins with the same invitation. Before we talk about repentance, discipline, or sacrifice, Jesus asks us to pause and consider what we truly want.

Desire is the doorway to discipleship. The disciples could have answered with something small or safe. Instead, they asked where He was staying—a way of saying, *"We want to be with You."* Lent is a season for clarifying our longings, stripping away the noise, and listening for the deeper ache beneath our surface wants.

Jesus does not ask, "What should you be seeking?" or "What do you think I want you to say?" He asks what is actually stirring in your heart. Lent is not about pretending to be holier than we are. It is about honesty—the kind that opens us to transformation.

Ash Wednesday reminds us of our mortality, but it also reminds us of our hunger. Dust returns to dust, but desire

3

reaches for God. The ashes on our foreheads are not only a sign of repentance; they are a confession that we long for something more than what this world can offer.

Jesus begins with a question because He wants relationship, not performance. He wants you to bring your real self, not your polished answers. Lent is His invitation to walk with Him, to dwell where He dwells, and to let your deepest desires lead you toward Him.

Encouragement: Christ welcomes your honest longing.

Reflection: What are you truly seeking as you begin this Lenten journey?

Thursday, February 19

"Why do you call me 'Lord, Lord' and not do what I say?"
(Luke 6:46)

J esus asks this question not to shame but to awaken. The crowds around Him admired His teaching. They called Him "Lord" with their lips, yet their lives remained unchanged. Lent begins by inviting us to examine the gap between confession and obedience.

We often call Jesus "Lord" because we believe it, or because it feels right, or because it's part of our spiritual vocabulary. But Jesus presses deeper: *Does your life reflect the One you name?* This is not a demand for perfection. It is an invitation to integrity, to let our actions align with our devotion.

Obedience in Scripture is not rigid compliance; it is trust expressed in practice. When Jesus asks this question, He is inviting us to build our lives on rock rather than sand. Lent is a season for noticing where our foundations have shifted, where we've drifted into convenience or habit rather than wholehearted following.

Jesus's question is tender but direct. He wants us to experience the freedom that comes from living truthfully—from letting our "Lord" be more than a title. Lent is not about earning His favor; it is about responding to His love with a life that reflects it.

Encouragement: Christ invites you into a life of honest alignment.

Reflection: Where is there a gap between what you profess and how you live?

Friday, February 20

"Do you want to be healed?" (John 5:6)

At the pool of Bethesda, Jesus approaches a man who has been ill for thirty-eight years. Instead of immediately healing him, Jesus asks a surprising question: *"Do you want to be healed?"* It seems obvious—who wouldn't want healing? Yet Jesus knows that healing requires change, and change can be frightening.

Sometimes we grow accustomed to our wounds. They become familiar, even defining. We may long for healing, yet resist the transformation it brings. Jesus's question invites honesty: *Do you truly desire wholeness, or have you settled into what is familiar?*

Lent is a season for naming the places where we've grown stuck—patterns, fears, habits, or hurts that feel immovable. Jesus does not force healing upon us. He invites us to participate, to desire, to say yes.

The man at the pool offers excuses, but Jesus meets him with compassion. Healing begins not with perfect faith but with willingness. Lent invites us to bring our hesitant yes, our fragile desire, our longing mixed with fear.

Jesus's question is not about worthiness but readiness. He stands before us with the same invitation: *Do you want to be healed?* Not someday. Not when conditions improve. Now.

Encouragement: Christ meets your desire for healing with compassion.

Reflection: Where do you long for healing, and what holds you back from embracing it?

Saturday, February 21

"Who touched me?" (Luke 8:45)

In the crowd, a woman reaches out to touch the hem of Jesus's garment. She hopes to remain unnoticed, to receive healing quietly. But Jesus stops and asks, *"Who touched me?"* His question is not about information; it is about relationship.

The woman wanted healing without being seen. Jesus wanted her to know she was seen. Lent invites us to move from anonymity to encounter—from reaching for God in secret to allowing ourselves to be known by Him.

Jesus's question draws the woman out of hiding. She comes trembling, unsure how He will respond. But Jesus calls her "daughter" and affirms her faith. His question reveals His heart: He does not merely dispense miracles; He restores dignity.

We often approach God hoping for help but fearing exposure. We want His power but hesitate to trust His tenderness. Jesus's question invites us to step into the light, to let ourselves be fully known and fully loved.

Lent is a season for letting God's gaze meet our need. Not to shame us, but to restore us. Jesus asks, *"Who touched me?"* because He wants connection, not secrecy.

Encouragement: Christ welcomes your reaching.
Reflection: Where are you tempted to hide needs from God?

Sunday, February 22

"Who do you say I am?" (*Matt. 16:15*)

J esus asks His disciples a question that cuts to the heart of discipleship: *"Who do you say I am?"* Not who others say He is, not what the crowds think, but what they believe.

Lent brings us to this question again and again. Our answer shapes everything—how we pray, how we trust, how we live. Peter answers, "You are the Christ," but even he does not yet grasp what that means. Jesus receives his confession and continues to lead him into deeper understanding.

Our confession may also be incomplete. We may say Jesus is Lord, Savior, Shepherd, or Teacher—yet still be learning what those names require of us. Jesus does not demand perfect theology; He invites honest confession and ongoing discovery.

Lent is a season for clarifying our answer. Who is Jesus to you today? Who is He becoming as you walk with Him? His question is not a test but an invitation to relationship.

Encouragement: Christ receives your confession and deepens your understanding.

Reflection: Who do you say Jesus is at this point in your journey?

Monday, February 23

"Do you believe this?" (John 11:26)

J esus speaks these words to Martha at her brother's tomb. Grief hangs heavy in the air. Hope feels impossible. Yet Jesus asks her to trust Him when nothing makes sense.

Faith is rarely tested in calm seasons. It is tested at the edge of loss and unanswered questions. Jesus does not ask Martha whether she understands. He asks whether she believes. Does she trust him—even when the outcome is unclear?

Lent invites us to bring our grief, confusion, and longing into the presence of Christ. Faith is not pretending everything is fine. It is trusting that Jesus is present even when life feels broken. Martha's belief does not erase her sorrow, but it opens her to the possibility of resurrection.

Jesus meets us in the same way. He does not demand certainty. He invites trust—trust in His character, His compassion, His timing. Lent is a season for letting our belief deepen, not by ignoring our pain, but by bringing it honestly to Him.

Encouragement: Christ comforts with a promise of life.

Reflection: Where is Jesus inviting you to trust Him in a place of sorrow or uncertainty?

Tuesday, February 24

"What do you want me to do for you?" (Mark 10:51)

J esus asks this question of a blind man crying out for mercy. It is a question of dignity. Jesus does not assume. He invites the man to name his desire.

Desire is holy ground. It reveals what we long for beneath our habits and fears. Lent invites us to listen to our desires—not to indulge them blindly, but to let them guide us toward God's healing and truth.

When Jesus asks, *"What do you want me to do for you?"* He is not offering a blank check. He is inviting relationship. He wants us to speak honestly, to bring our longings into the light, to trust that He cares about what we carry.

Sometimes we silence our desires because they feel too big, too small, or too complicated. But Jesus welcomes them. He meets us where our longing is most tender.

Lent is a season for naming what we truly want—not what we think we should want, but what our hearts actually ache for. Jesus listens without judgment.

Encouragement: Christ welcomes your honest desires.

Reflection: What do you want Jesus to do for you?

Wednesday, February 25

"Why do you worry about your life?" (Matt. 6:25)

J esus asks this question in the middle of a teaching about trust. He points to birds and flowers—small, ordinary things—as reminders of God's attentive care. His question is not a dismissal of our concerns but an invitation to see our lives through a different lens.

Worry narrows our vision. It convinces us that everything depends on us. Jesus's question gently loosens our grip. He invites us to know that we are held, provided for, and loved.

Lent is a season for noticing the worries that shape our days—the quiet anxieties that drain our energy and cloud our perspective. Jesus does not shame us for worrying. He invites us to shift our focus from scarcity to trust.

Worry often grows from the illusion of control. Jesus's question reminds us that our lives are rooted in God's faithfulness, not our own striving. Lent teaches us to release our burdens and to rest in the One who knows our needs before we speak.

Encouragement: Christ invites you to rest in God's care.

Reflection: What worry is weighing on you today, and how might you release it into God's hands?

Thursday, February 26

"What good is it to gain the whole world?" (Mark 8:36)

J esus asks this question to expose the illusions that often guide our choices. The world promises success, security, and recognition—yet none of these can satisfy the soul. Lent invites us to examine what we are pursuing and why.

We can gain much and still feel empty. We can achieve our goals and still feel restless. Jesus's question cuts through the noise: *What is the value of all you chase if it costs you your soul?*

This is not a threat; it is a wake-up call. Jesus wants us to live with clarity, not regret. He invites us to consider what truly matters—what endures, what brings life, what aligns with God's heart.

Lent is a season for reordering our loves. It is a time to release what distracts us and to hold fast to what nourishes us. Jesus's question helps us see the difference between what is urgent and what is essential.

Encouragement: Christ invites you to pursue what truly gives life.

Reflection: What are you chasing that may be costing you more than it gives?

Friday, February 27

"Can you drink the cup I drink?" (Mark 10:38)

James and John ask Jesus for places of honor. Jesus responds with a question that reveals the cost of discipleship: *"Can you drink the cup I drink?"* Following Him is not about status but surrender.

The "cup" Jesus speaks of is the path of self-giving love—a path marked by humility, sacrifice, and trust. Lent invites us to consider what it means to follow Jesus not only in His glory but also in His suffering.

We often want the blessings of discipleship without the cost. Jesus's question invites us to a deeper, more honest commitment. He does not ask us to seek suffering, but to be willing to love in ways that may cost us something.

The cup Jesus drinks is ultimately the cup of obedience to the Father's will. Lent teaches us to say yes to God even when the path is difficult or unclear.

Encouragement: Christ strengthens you to follow Him with courage.

Reflection: What part of following Jesus feels costly for you right now?

Saturday, February 28

"Why are you thinking these things in your hearts?" (Luke 5:22)

J esus asks this question when the religious leaders silently judge Him for forgiving a paralyzed man. They never speak their criticism aloud, yet Jesus knows their thoughts. His question reveals that He cares not only about our actions but also about the inner movements of our hearts.

Lent invites us to pay attention to our interior life—the quiet assumptions, judgments, fears, and motives that shape our responses. We often focus on outward behavior, but Jesus looks deeper. He invites us to notice what is stirring beneath the surface.

His question is not accusatory. It is diagnostic. It helps us see what we might otherwise ignore. Our hearts are shaped by many things: past wounds, unspoken fears, hidden pride, unexamined beliefs. Jesus's question invites us to bring these inner currents into the light of His grace.

Lent is a season for honest self-examination, not self-condemnation. Jesus asks this question to free us, not to shame us. He wants our hearts to be aligned with His love.

Encouragement: Christ gently reveals what needs healing within you.

Reflection: What thoughts or inner reactions is Jesus inviting you to notice today?

Sunday, March 1

"Do you still not understand?" (Mark 8:21)

J esus asks this question after the disciples misunderstand
His teaching yet again. Their confusion frustrates them,
but Jesus remains patient. His question is not a scolding;
it is an invitation to deeper perception.

Understanding grows slowly. The disciples had seen miracles,
heard parables, and walked closely with Jesus—yet they still
struggled to grasp His meaning. Lent reminds us that spiritual
growth is a gradual unfolding, not a sudden leap.

Jesus's question invites us to pay attention, to look beneath
the surface, to let our hearts be shaped by His presence. He
does not demand instant clarity. He invites ongoing openness.

We often want quick answers. Jesus wants relationship. Lent
teaches us to sit with His words, to let them work on us over
time, to trust that understanding will come as we walk with
Him.

Encouragement: Christ is patient with your slow-growing
understanding.

Reflection: Where is Jesus inviting you to slow down and
listen more deeply?

Monday, March 2

"Why did you doubt?" (Matt. 14:31)

Peter steps out of the boat with boldness, walking toward Jesus on the water. But when the wind rises, fear overtakes him. As he sinks, Jesus reaches out His hand and asks, *"Why did you doubt?"* The question is not a reprimand. It is an invitation to notice what shifted inside him.

Doubt often enters quietly. It begins when we take our eyes off Jesus and fix them on the storm. Lent invites us to see the subtle ways fear replaces trust.

Peter's doubt did not disqualify him. Jesus still reached for him. Still saved him. Still called him forward. Doubt is not the opposite of faith; it is part of the journey of learning to trust. Jesus's question helps Peter see where his confidence faltered so that his faith can grow.

Lent is a season for noticing what pulls our attention away from Christ. Jesus meets us in those moments with compassion, not judgment.

Encouragement: Christ reaches out when doubt rises.

Reflection: What fear or distraction most often pulls your attention away from Jesus?

Tuesday, March 3

"Do you love me?" (John 21:17)

After the resurrection, Jesus asks Peter three times, *"Do you love me?"* The repetition mirrors Peter's three denials, not to shame him but to restore him. Jesus's question is tender, personal, and healing.

Love is the foundation of discipleship. Before Jesus sends Peter to feed His sheep, He asks about love. Not competence. Not courage. Not readiness. Love. Lent invites us to return to this foundation—to remember that our life with Christ begins not with our performance but with our affection.

Jesus's question is not about proving anything. It is about honesty. Peter answers with humility: *"Lord, you know everything; you know that I love you."* His love is imperfect, but real. Jesus receives it and entrusts him with purpose.

Lent is a season for letting Jesus restore what has been fractured—our confidence, our calling, our sense of belonging. His question draws us back our relationship with Him.

Encouragement: Christ receives your imperfect love and restores your calling.

Reflection: How would you answer Jesus's question?

Wednesday, March 4

"Why are you sleeping?" (Luke 22:46)

In Gethsemane, Jesus finds His disciples asleep during His hour of anguish. He asks, *"Why are you sleeping?"* The question is not about physical rest. It is about spiritual wakefulness.

We, too, fall asleep in crucial moments—not literally, but spiritually. We become numb, distracted, overwhelmed, or disengaged. Lent invites us to wake up, to stay present to God's movement in our lives, to resist spiritual drowsiness.

Jesus's question is gentle but urgent. He knows the disciples are exhausted with sorrow. He knows the weight they carry. Yet He calls them to watchfulness—not out of duty, but because wakefulness is the posture that prepares us to receive God's strength.

Lent is a season for noticing where we've grown dull or inattentive. Jesus does not scold us for our weariness. He invites us to rise, to pray, to stay awake to His presence.

Encouragement: Christ calls you back to wakefulness.

Reflection: Where have you grown spiritually sleepy, and what might help you wake up?

22

Thursday, March 5

"Why do you look for the living among the dead?" (*Luke 24:5*)

T he women come to the tomb carrying spices, expecting to tend to a dead body. Instead, they are met by angels who ask, *"Why do you look for the living among the dead?"* It is a question that redirects their expectations and opens their eyes to resurrection.

We often return to places of disappointment, regret, or old patterns expecting to find life there. Lent invites us to notice where we are searching for hope in places that cannot give it.

The angels' question is not a rebuke. It is a revelation. It invites the women—and us—to lift our gaze from what is finished to what God is making new. Resurrection is not found in the tombs of our past but in the living presence of Christ.

Lent prepares us for this shift. It teaches us to release what is dead and to look for signs of life where God is already at work.

Encouragement: Christ invites you to seek life where He is present, not where hope has faded.

Reflection: Where might you be searching for life in places that cannot offer it?

Friday, March 6

"Why do you see the speck in your brother's eye?" (Matt. 7:3)

Jesus asks this question to expose our tendency toward judgment. We notice the faults of others with sharp clarity while overlooking our own. His question is not meant to shame but to redirect our attention inward.

Lent is a season for humility. It invites us to examine our own hearts before critiquing others. Jesus's question helps us see how we use comparison to avoid our own brokenness.

The goal is not self-condemnation but self-awareness. When we recognize our own need for grace, we become more compassionate. Jesus invites us to remove the log from our own eye so that we can see clearly—not to judge, but to love.

Lent teaches us that transformation begins within. Jesus's question helps us shift from blame to honesty, from criticism to compassion.

Encouragement: Christ invites you to see yourself and others with grace.

Reflection: Where are you tempted to judge others instead of examining your own heart?

Saturday, March 7

"Do you understand what I have done for you?" (John 13:12)

After washing His disciples' feet, Jesus asks them, *"Do you understand what I have done for you?"* It is a question that invites reflection, not immediate answers. The disciples have witnessed humility so unexpected they can barely take it in.

Jesus is not simply teaching them to serve. He is revealing the shape of His love—a love that kneels, a love that stoops, a love that gives itself away. Lent invites us to sit with this question, to let it unsettle us, to let it open our eyes to the kind of love Jesus calls us to embody.

Understanding, in Scripture, is not merely intellectual. It is lived. Jesus wants His disciples to grasp the meaning of His actions so they can imitate them. He wants people who serve not out of obligation but out of love.

Lent is a season for letting Jesus reshape our understanding of greatness. His question invites us to follow his example.

Encouragement: Christ teaches you humility and love.

Reflection: What is Jesus inviting you to imitate?

Sunday, March 8

"Which of these was a neighbor?" (*Luke 10:36*)

J esus tells of a man beaten and left on the roadside, passed by by "religious" people expected to help, until a Samaritan— an outsider—stops, tends his wounds, and ensures his care. In the story, mercy becomes the true measure of a neighbor.

Jesus's question invites us to consider not only the Samaritan's compassion but the posture of a heart shaped by mercy. Being a neighbor is not a task to complete but a way of seeing. It is a willingness to be interrupted, to be moved, to respond.

Lent invites us to let this question shape our week: not "Who deserves my care?" but "How can I reflect God's mercy today?" Jesus's question becomes a compass, guiding us toward a life marked by compassion.

Encouragement: Christ forms your heart to reflect His compassion and mercy.

Reflection: How might you practice mercy and the love of neighbor in your life?

Monday, March 9

"Why do you call me good?" (Mark 10:18)

A man runs up to Jesus, eager and sincere, calling Him "Good Teacher." Jesus responds with a question that seems to deflect the compliment: *"Why do you call me good?"* He is not denying His goodness. He is inviting the man to examine what he means by the word.

We often use spiritual language without fully considering its weight. Jesus's question invites us to move from flattery to truth, from surface admiration to genuine recognition. Lent is a season for aligning our hearts with our words.

The man wants eternal life, but he also wants to keep control. Jesus's question exposes the tension between his desire for God and his attachment to his possessions. Lent invites us to notice our own divided loyalties.

Jesus's question is not a rebuke. It is an invitation to clarity. He wants the man—and us—to understand who He truly is and what following Him truly means.

Encouragement: Christ invites you into honesty about who He is and what you desire.

Reflection: How willing are you to follow Him?

Tuesday, March 10

"Why do you test me?" (Matt. 22:18)

Religious leaders approach Jesus with a question designed to trap Him: "Is it lawful to pay taxes to Caesar?" If He says "Yes, pay the tax," the crowds will see Him as a Roman sympathizer; if He says "No," they can report Him to Rome for rebellion.

Jesus sees through their motives and asks, *"Why do you test me?"* His question exposes the gap between their outward religiosity and their inward intentions. His answer, of course, finds a third way: *"Render unto Caesar what is Caesar's and to God what is God's."*

Lent invites us to examine not only what we do, but why we do it. Our motives matter. We can pray, serve, or give for reasons that have little to do with love. Jesus's question helps us notice when our actions are driven by fear, pride, or self-protection rather than trust.

Testing God often looks like withholding trust until He proves Himself. It is the posture of a guarded heart. Jesus invites us to move from suspicion to surrender, from testing to trusting.

His question is not meant to shame us. It is meant to free us from the exhausting work of managing outcomes and controlling appearances. Lent is a season for letting God purify our motives so that our actions flow from love.

Encouragement: Christ invites you to bring your motives into the light of His grace.

Reflection: Where might you be testing God instead of trusting Him?

Wednesday, March 11

"Why are you troubled, and why do doubts rise in your minds?" (Luke 24:38)

After the resurrection, Jesus appears to His disciples, and they are startled and afraid. He asks them, *"Why are you troubled, and why do doubts rise in your minds?"* His question acknowledges their fear while inviting them into peace.

Trouble and doubt often rise unbidden. They come from past wounds, unmet expectations, or the shock of encountering God in ways we did not anticipate. Jesus's question is not a reprimand. It is a gentle invitation to bring our confusion into His presence.

Lent is a season for noticing what unsettles us. Jesus does not ask us to suppress our doubts. He asks us to face them with Him. His presence transforms fear into understanding, confusion into clarity, and doubt into deeper trust.

The disciples' trouble came from not yet recognizing the fullness of who Jesus was. Lent invites us to see Him more clearly, to let His presence calm our fears, steady our hearts, and live with compassion and love.

Encouragement: Christ meets your trouble with His peace.

Reflection: What doubts or troubles are rising in your mind today, and how might Jesus be inviting you to bring them to Him?

Thursday, March 12

"Why are you thinking these things?" (Mark 2:8)

When Jesus forgives a paralyzed man, the religious leaders silently question His authority. Jesus responds with a question that reveals He sees beyond their thoughts to the deeper posture of their hearts.

Lent invites us to examine the thoughts that shape our reactions—those quick judgments, quiet assumptions, or hidden fears that influence how we see God and others. Jesus's question is not accusatory. It is an invitation to awareness.

Our thoughts often reveal our deepest beliefs: about God's character, about our worth, about what is possible. Jesus wants to free us from the patterns that keep us stuck—patterns of cynicism, suspicion, or self-protection.

His question invites us to bring our inner world into His light, trusting that He meets us with compassion, not condemnation.

Encouragement: Christ gently reveals the thoughts that need His healing.

Reflection: What recurring thoughts might Jesus be inviting you to examine more closely?

Friday, March 13

"Why are you so afraid?" (Mark 4:40)

This is a different moment from the earlier "Why are you afraid?" In this scene, Jesus has just calmed a violent storm. The disciples are overwhelmed—not only by the storm, but by the power Jesus reveals.

Fear often arises when God acts in ways we do not expect. The disciples feared the storm, but they also feared the One who commanded it. Jesus's question invites them to move from fear of circumstances to awe of His presence.

Lent teaches us that fear can be a doorway to deeper faith. When we encounter God's power, we are reminded that He is not small, predictable, or manageable. He is Lord over all.

Jesus's question is not a rebuke. It is an invitation to trust the One who holds authority over every storm—both around us and within us.

Encouragement: Christ invites you to let awe replace fear.

Reflection: Where is God inviting you to trust His power rather than fear it?

Saturday, March 14

"Why do you entertain evil thoughts?" (Matt. 9:4)

Jesus asks this question when He perceives the unspoken resistance of those who doubt His authority to forgive. His question is not about moral policing. It is about the inner movements that shape our outward lives.

Lent invites us to notice the thoughts we entertain—those that diminish others, distort our view of God, or undermine our own sense of worth. Jesus's question is meant to awaken us to the subtle ways our hearts drift from love.

Evil thoughts are not always dramatic. Sometimes they are quiet resentments, lingering judgments, or hidden fears. Jesus invites us to bring these into His light so that He can heal what lies beneath them.

His question is an invitation to honesty, humility, and transformation.

Encouragement: Christ invites you to bring even your hidden thoughts into His healing presence.

Reflection: What inner attitudes might Jesus be inviting you to release?

Sunday, March 15

"Why do you doubt?" (Luke 24:28)

When the risen Jesus appears to His disciples, they are startled, overwhelmed, and unsure what to believe. His first words are peace, and His first question is gentle: *"Why do you doubt?"* He is not scolding them. He is naming the tension between what they hoped for and what they can barely imagine is true.

Doubt often rises in the space between promise and fulfillment. The disciples had heard Jesus speak of resurrection, yet the reality of it was almost too much to take in. Lent invites us to acknowledge the places where hope feels fragile, where belief and uncertainty coexist.

Jesus does not demand instant clarity. He offers His presence. He shows His hands and feet. He eats with them. He meets their doubt with reassurance. Lent teaches us that faith grows not by suppressing doubt, but by bringing it honestly into the presence of Christ.

His question is an invitation to trust the One who stands before us—alive, patient, and full of peace. Through His sacrifice, He shows us how to love with our own acts of love.

Encouragement: Christ meets your doubt with His living presence.

Reflection: Where is Jesus inviting you to trust Him even before you fully understand?

Monday, March 16

"Why do you break the command of God for the sake of your tradition?" (Matt. 15:3)

J esus asks this question to expose how easily religious practices can drift from their purpose. Traditions can be beautiful, but they can also become barriers when they overshadow the heart of God's commands.

Lent invites us to examine the habits, routines, and assumptions that shape our spiritual lives. Are they drawing us closer to God, or are they keeping us from seeing Him clearly?

Jesus's question is not an attack on tradition. It is an invitation to return to the heart of God's law—love of God and love of neighbor. When our practices lose sight of this, Jesus gently calls us back.

Encouragement: Christ invites you to return to what matters most.

Reflection: What spiritual habits might need to be re-examined in this season?

Tuesday, March 17

"Why do you ask me about what is good?" (*Matt. 19:17*)

A rich young man approaches Jesus with a sincere question about goodness. Jesus responds by challenging his assumptions. Goodness is not a checklist. It is a relationship with the One who is truly good.

Lent invites us to move beyond moral performance toward deeper intimacy with God. Jesus's question exposes the man's desire for clarity without surrender, for righteousness without relationship.

Jesus invites him—and us—to see goodness not as something we achieve, but as something we receive through walking with Him.

Encouragement: Christ invites you into a goodness rooted in relationship, not performance.

Reflection: Where might you be seeking spiritual achievement instead of deeper connection with God?

Wednesday, March 18

"Why do you not judge for yourselves what is right?" (*Luke 12:57*)

Jesus asks this question to challenge His listeners to take responsibility for their discernment. They rely on external authorities while ignoring the inner witness of truth.

Lent invites us to cultivate spiritual discernment—to listen for God's voice, to weigh our choices carefully, and to act with integrity. Jesus's question calls us to maturity, to move beyond passive faith into active wisdom.

He is not asking us to rely on ourselves alone. He is inviting us to engage our hearts and minds in partnership with His Spirit.

Encouragement: Christ invites you to grow in discernment and wisdom.

Reflection: Where is Jesus inviting you to judge rightly and act with integrity?

Thursday, March 19

"Why do you call me 'Lord, Lord' and not do what I say?"
(Luke 6:46)

This question appeared earlier in Lent, but here it takes on a different angle. Jesus is not repeating Himself. He is deepening the invitation.

Calling Jesus "Lord" is easy. Following Him is costly. Lent invites us to examine the places where our obedience lags behind our confession, where our intentions outpace our actions.

Jesus's question is not condemnation. It is a call to alignment—to let our lives reflect the One we name as Lord.

Encouragement: Christ invites you into a life where your actions reflect your devotion.

Reflection: Where is Jesus inviting you to take a concrete step of obedience?

Friday, March 20

"Why do you think evil in your hearts?" (Matt. 9:4)

Jesus asks this question when He perceives the hidden resistance of those who doubt His authority. It is a question that reveals His concern for the inner life.

Lent invites us to examine the subtle ways our hearts drift—toward cynicism, resentment, or fear. Jesus's question is not meant to shame us. It is meant to awaken us to the thoughts that shape our lives.

He invites us to bring even our hidden struggles into His healing presence.

Encouragement: Christ invites you to let His grace transform your inner life.

Reflection: What hidden attitudes might Jesus be inviting you to surrender?

Saturday, March 21

"Why do you not understand my language?" (John 8:43)

J esus asks this question to reveal the deeper issue beneath His listeners' confusion: they hear His words, but they do not receive them. Understanding requires openness, humility, and willingness to be changed.

Lent invites us to listen not only with our ears but with our hearts. Jesus's question challenges us to consider what keeps us from hearing Him clearly—distraction, fear, pride, or simply the noise of our lives.

He speaks a language of love, truth, and freedom. To understand Him, we must be willing to let His words shape us.

Encouragement: Christ invites you to listen with openness and humility.

Reflection: What might be keeping you from hearing Jesus clearly?

Sunday, March 22

"Why do you not understand what I say?" (John 8:43)

T his Sunday's question echoes Saturday's but takes a different angle. Jesus is not frustrated. He is inviting His listeners to recognize the barriers that keep them from receiving His words.

Lent is a season for clearing away those barriers—distraction, resistance, fear—so that we can hear Jesus more clearly. His question invites us to deeper openness and greater trust.

Encouragement: Christ patiently teaches you to hear His voice.

Reflection: What is Jesus inviting you to understand more deeply this week?

Monday, March 23

"Why are you trying to kill me?" (John 7:19)

J esus asks this question in the temple courts, confronting the hostility that has been building around Him. His words expose the tension between outward religiosity and inward resistance. The people claim to honor God, yet they reject the One sent by God.

Lent invites us to examine the subtle ways we resist Jesus's authority. We may not oppose Him openly, but we sometimes cling to control, comfort, or certainty in ways that push Him to the margins. His question is not an accusation. It is an invitation to honesty.

Jesus names the truth not to condemn but to free. He wants His listeners—and us—to see the ways fear, pride, or misunderstanding can harden the heart. Lent is a season for letting His truth soften us, awaken us, and draw us back to Him.

Encouragement: Christ invites you to bring even your resistance into His light.

Reflection: Where might you be resisting Jesus's work in your life?

Tuesday, March 24

"Why do you not understand what I say?" (John 8:43)

J esus asks this question to reveal the deeper barriers that keep His listeners from receiving His words. Understanding is not merely intellectual. It requires openness, humility, and a willingness to be changed.

Lent invites us to listen beneath the surface—to hear not only Jesus's words but His heart. Sometimes we struggle to understand because His teaching challenges our assumptions or calls us beyond what feels comfortable.

Jesus's question is not frustration. It is invitation. He wants us to recognize the obstacles that keep us from hearing Him clearly so that He can remove them.

Encouragement: Christ patiently teaches you to hear His voice.

Reflection: What might be keeping you from receiving Jesus's words with openness?

Wednesday, March 25

"I showed you many good works. For which are you trying to stone me?" (John 10:32)

Jesus asks this question after performing works of compassion and healing. His listeners respond not with gratitude but with hostility. His question exposes the disconnect between their stated devotion to God and their rejection of God's work in their midst.

Lent invites us to consider the ways we resist what God is doing—especially when it challenges our expectations. Sometimes God's grace disrupts our categories. Sometimes His mercy unsettles our assumptions.

Jesus's question is not self-pity. It is revelation. He wants His listeners to see the contradiction in their response so they can turn toward truth.

Encouragement: Christ invites you to recognize and release the resistance that rises when He works in unexpected ways.

Reflection: Where might God be acting in your life in ways that unsettle you?

Thursday, March 26

"Why do you not believe me?" (John 8:46)

J esus asks this question to reveal the heart of unbelief. His words and works testify to who He is, yet many refuse to trust Him. Their unbelief is not due to lack of evidence but to a closed heart.

Lent invites us to examine the places where belief comes slowly—where fear, disappointment, or past wounds make trust difficult. Jesus's question is not a demand for perfect faith. It is an invitation to bring our hesitations into His presence.

Belief grows through relationship. Jesus invites us to trust Him not because we understand everything, but because He is faithful.

Encouragement: Christ meets your hesitant belief with patience and grace.

Reflection: Where is Jesus inviting you to trust Him more deeply?

Friday, March 27

"Why are you bothering this woman?" (Matt. 26:10)

When a woman anoints Jesus with costly perfume, others criticize her. Jesus intervenes with a question that defends her devotion and exposes their misunderstanding: *"Why are you bothering this woman?"*

Lent invites us to consider how easily we judge the expressions of devotion we do not understand. Jesus sees the heart behind the act. He honors the love that others dismiss.

His question challenges us to release our need to control how others worship, serve, or express their faith. It invites us to see with compassion rather than criticism.

Encouragement: Christ honors the love you offer Him, even when others do not understand.

Reflection: Where might Jesus be inviting you to show grace rather than judgment?

Saturday, March 28

"Why are you sleeping?" (Luke 22:46)

I n Gethsemane, Jesus finds His disciples asleep during His hour of anguish. His question is both tender and urgent. He knows their exhaustion, yet He calls them to wakefulness.

Lent invites us to notice where we have grown spiritually drowsy—where distraction, weariness, or avoidance have dulled our awareness of God's presence. Jesus's question is not condemnation. It is invitation.

He calls us to stay awake with Him, to be present to His suffering, and to prepare our hearts for the path ahead.

Encouragement: Christ gently calls you back to wakefulness and presence.

Reflection: Where have you grown spiritually sleepy, and how might Jesus be inviting you to awaken?

Palm Sunday, March 29

"Why are you doing this?" (Mark 11:3)

As Jesus enters Jerusalem, He sends two disciples to fetch a colt. He tells them that if anyone asks why they are taking it, they should answer, *"The Lord needs it."* The question—*"Why are you doing this?"*—permeates Holy Week.

Palm Sunday invites us to consider our own motivations for following Jesus. Are we drawn by hope? By habit? By longing? By fear? The crowds welcomed Him with shouts of praise, yet many misunderstood the kind of King He was.

Jesus enters not with force but with humility. Not to conquer Rome but to conquer death. His question invites us to examine the intentions behind our discipleship.

Lent has been a journey of questions—questions that reveal, invite, challenge, and heal. Palm Sunday gathers them into a single invitation: follow the One who comes in humility, who knows your heart, and who leads you toward life.

Encouragement: Christ welcomes your honest motives and invites you to follow Him with a whole heart.

Reflection: Why are you following Jesus into this Holy Week, and what do you hope to discover?

Closing Thoughts

Lent is a season of questions—forty days shaped not by our answers, but by the voice of Jesus calling us deeper. His questions have invited honesty, awakened desire, exposed fear, revealed resistance, and opened our hearts to grace. They have not been tests to pass, but doorways into relationship.

As you move beyond this season, carry these questions with you. Let them echo in your prayer, your choices, your relationships, your hopes. Jesus's questions are not confined to Lent. They are invitations that continue to shape us long after the season ends.

He asks because He loves. He questions because He wants to draw you near. He speaks because He desires your freedom.

The journey of Lent leads us toward the cross, but it does not end there. It leads us to the empty tomb, to the risen Christ who still calls us by name, who still asks us what we seek, who still invites us to follow Him into life.

May these questions continue to guide you. May His presence continue to steady you. And may the One who has walked with you through this season lead you into the joy and hope of resurrection.